RECRUITING & TRAINING

SUCCESSFUL SUBSTITUTE TEACHERS

CORWIN
PRESS

The Corwin Press logo — a raven striding across an open book — represents the happy union of courage and learning. We are a professional-level publisher of books and journals for K–12 educators, and we are committed to creating and providing resources that embody these qualities. Corwin's motto is "Success for All Learners."

RECRUITING & TRAINING SUCCESSFUL SUBSTITUTE TEACHERS

James B. Rowley, Ph.D.
Patricia M. Hart, Ph.D.

For information address:

 Corwin Press, Inc.
A Sage Publications Company
2455 Teller Road
Thousand Oaks, California 91320
E-mail: order@corwinpress.com

SAGE Publications Ltd.
6 Bonhill Street
London EC2A 4PU
United Kingdom

SAGE Publications India Pvt. Ltd.
M-32 Market
Greater Kailash I
New Delhi 110 048 India

ISBN 0-8039-6775-6

This book is printed on acid-free paper.

01 02 03 10 9 8 7 6 5 4 3 2

Production Editor: S. Marlene Head
Editorial Assistant: Kristen L. Gibson

Contents

About the Developers

Recruiting & Training Successful Substitute Teachers was created and coproduced by James Rowley and Patricia Hart of the University of Dayton. Jim and Tricia collaborated to produce the Corwin Press audiotape series *Becoming a Star Teacher: Practical Strategies and Inspiration for K-6 Teachers* (1997). Other video-based teacher training programs produced by Jim and Tricia include *Mentoring the New Teacher* (1993) and *Becoming a Star Urban Teacher* (1995), both in national distribution through the Association of Supervision and Curriculum Development (ASCD). Jim and Tricia are dedicated to using audio and video technologies to capture and communicate the knowledge and wisdom of classroom teachers. In 1993, and again in 1995, they were corecipients of the Distinguished Research in Teacher Education award presented annually by the national Association of Teacher Educators (ATE).

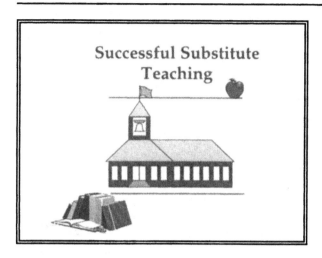

Module 1

**Substitute Teaching
Hopes and Concerns**

Personal Survey

Instructions

On the Post-it notes provided at your table, answer the two questions that appear on the next slide.

You may provide more than one response for each question.

Each response should be on a different Post-it note.

Survey Questions

1. What is the major concern you have about substitute teaching?

2. What do you hope to gain from your experience as a substitute teacher?

Reminder: You may have more than one response for each question, but each response must be on a separate Post-it note.

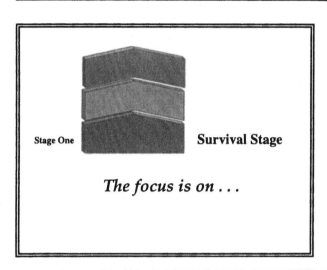

The key questions are:

* Will I make it?
* How am I doing?
* Do others approve of my performance?

Stage Two   **Task Stage**

Stage One   **Survival Stage**

The focus is on . . .

Time and Task

The key questions are:

* How can I manage to do all that is expected of me?
* Am I doing it right?
* Is there a better way?

Stage Three

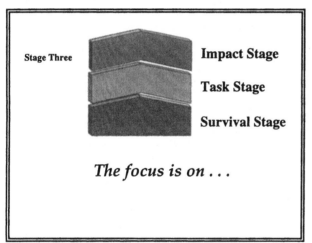

Impact Stage

Task Stage

Survival Stage

The focus is on . . .

Student Learning

The key questions are:

* Are students engaging the material?
* How can I raise achievement levels?
* Is this meaningful to students?

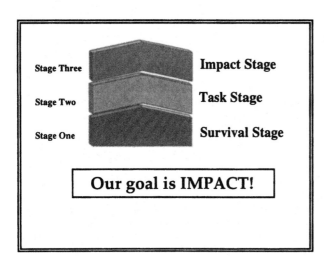

Our goal is IMPACT!

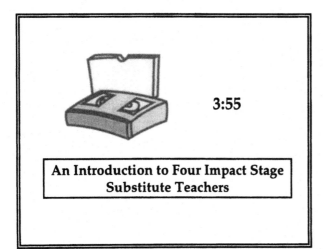

3:55

An Introduction to Four Impact Stage Substitute Teachers

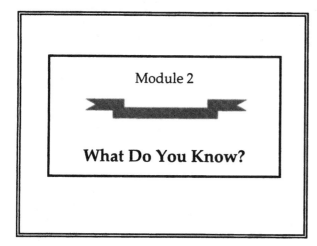

Module 2

What Do You Know?

What do you know?

   What do you want to know?

         About

   SUBSTITUTE TEACHING

An Introduction to:

The KWL Strategy

What I KNOW	What I WANT to Know	What I LEARNED

Substitute Teaching KWL

What I *Know* About Substitute Teaching	What I *Want* to Know About Substitute Teaching	What I *Learned* About Substitute Teaching

Module 2: What Do You Know?

The Four Performance Areas of Substitute Teachers	
Quadrant 1	Quadrant 3
Quadrant 2	Quadrant 4

The Four Performance Areas of Substitute Teachers	
Interpersonal Functions	Quadrant 3
Quadrant 2	Quadrant 4

The Four Performance Areas of Substitute Teachers	
Interpersonal Functions	Quadrant 3
Instructional Functions	Quadrant 4

The Four Performance Areas of Substitute Teachers	
Interpersonal Functions	Logistical Functions
Instructional Functions	Quadrant 4

The Four Performance Areas of Substitute Teachers	
Interpersonal Functions	Logistical Functions
Instructional Functions	Professional Functions

What Is a *Function*?

Function: **A performance-based criterion composed of a belief and a set of congruent behaviors**

For example . . .

Function 3C

3C: Ensuring that the physical environment of the classroom is left in a clean and orderly condition

---

Function 3C

Belief: I am a guest in the regular teacher's classroom. Guests should treat their host's home with respect.

Function 3C

Belief: I am a guest in the regular teacher's classroom. Guests should treat their host's home with respect.

Behavior: I reshelve materials and straighten the teacher's desk before leaving for the day.

Interpersonal Quadrant

Employing effective communication and human relations functions to build student-teacher relationships conducive to teaching and learning

Instructional Quadrant

Employing teaching functions designed to achieve stated objectives, maintain instructional flow, and promote student learning

Logistical Quadrant

Employing management functions aimed at the efficient delivery of services within the rules, norms, and codes of the workplace

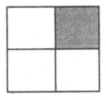

Professional Quadrant

Employing consultation and reflection functions consistent with professional practice and based on a respect for confidentiality

Processing your:

KWL on Substitute Teaching

What I KNOW	What I WANT to Know	What I LEARNED

Module 3

Reflections

Aha!

A moment of clarity and understanding, sudden insight, or perception

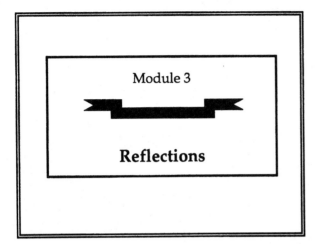

Oh No!

An unpleasant surprise or shock perhaps accentuated with disappointment or disillusionment

Aha!
A moment of clarity and understanding, sudden insight, or perception

Oh No!
An unpleasant surprise or shock perhaps accentuated with disappointment or disillusionment

Hmm?
A moment of curiosity and intensified interest characterized by a need for further reflection

Hmm?

A moment of curiosity and intensified interest characterized by a need for further reflection

On any given day, as many as 8% of a school's teachers are absent, requiring the services of a substitute teacher.

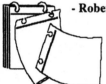

- Robert Warren, 1988, p. 96

. . . Substitutes are a major force in today's schools. Unfortunately, research tells us that they receive little support, no specialized training, and are rarely evaluated.

- Terrie St. Michel, 1995, p. 6

The average student spends 7 days out of every school year with a substitute teacher. That comes to 84 days (nearly half a school year) during 12 years of schooling.

- McIntire & Hughes, 1982, p. 702

In a survey of 1,728 school districts . . . 70% required no minimum professional training of substitutes and 97% required no previous teaching experience.

- C. H. Koelling, 1983, p. 163

Substituting is probably the most difficult and demanding job within the field of education and the one that receives the least amount of attention and support. Positive changes . . . will require a true team effort.

- Terrie St. Michael, 1995, p. 6

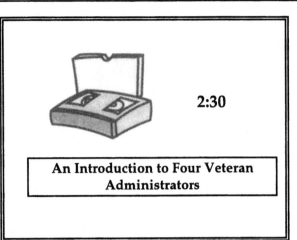

2:30

An Introduction to Four Veteran
Administrators

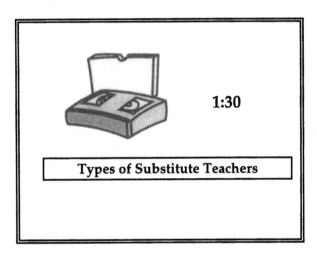

1:30

Types of Substitute Teachers

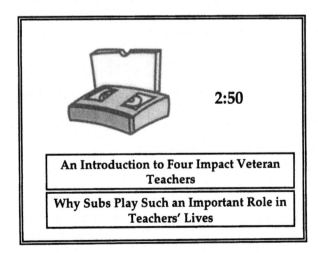

2:50

An Introduction to Four Impact Veteran
Teachers

Why Subs Play Such an Important Role in
Teachers' Lives

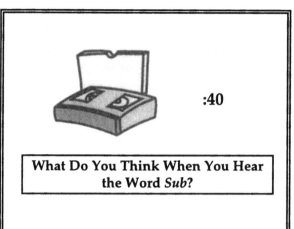

:40

What Do You Think When You Hear the Word *Sub*?

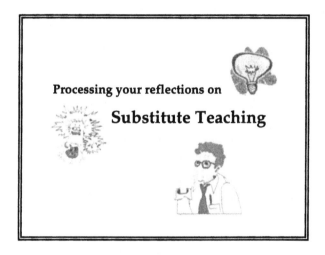

Processing your reflections on

Substitute Teaching

Module 4

First Impressions Last

Case Study #1

Instructions

1. Read the case and make personal notes on at least three things the substitute teacher could have done differently.

2. Discuss the case with your group and make a group list of at least ten things the sub could have done differently.

Processing your

Ideas on Enhancing Performance in

Quadrant 1

Case Study #1

Linda Preston was a recent graduate of a private university where she had majored in sociology. Following graduation, she was unable to find work in her hometown where she hoped to settle down in an apartment of her own. As the weeks passed, it became clear to Linda that she would have to do what she had hoped to avoid: take a part-time job to keep her afloat until she landed a full-time position.

Several days later, Linda had a backyard conversation with her parents' neighbor, Bill, an assistant principal at the local high school. Bill explained to Linda that the local schools were in desperate need of substitute teachers and that the work had many advantages. For one thing, subbing would afford her the flexibility to continue to search for a full-time position. After doing some rough calculations---$65.00 per day, 10 days per month---she decided to give substitute teaching a shot. After all, what did she have to lose?

Linda's first early morning call came just 2 days later. Her first assignment was to cover Mrs. Keating's 7th-grade American History class for 3 consecutive days. The teacher was fighting a serious flu bug, and the doctor had advised 3 days of rest.

Linda entered Room 231 just as the bell rang to announce the beginning of first period. The 32 junior high students were busy talking and laughing and seemed to hardly notice her entrance. Several students were out of their seats, so Linda said, "Okay, sit down please, and we'll get going with the assignment that Mrs. Keating left." Very few students sat down. "Come on, let's get going so we can get this over with." Only a couple of students turned her way. Again, she pleaded with the group: "I am sure Mrs. Keating wants you to keep up with your classwork." One of the students' books fell to the floor. In the next few minutes, it seemed like everyone's books were falling on the floor.

Linda picked up one of the books and slammed it on the desk of a student in the front row who had dropped it. This seemed to get their attention. "The next student's book that falls on the floor goes to the office." She turned her back to write the assignment on the board. The class felt like a powder keg waiting to explode, and she closed her eyes hoping it would not go off. Somebody slammed a book on their desk, and though she turned quickly, there was no way to know who had done it. Several students had their heads down on their desks trying to control their laughter. "Was that you, young man?" she demanded of one of the more guilty-looking students. "Oh, no. I am working on chapter six, see!" he said, indicating that his book was open and that he had a pen in his hand.

"Well, good. Everyone should be working on chapter six. If you complete the questions at the end of the chapter, I have a worksheet for you to do," Linda added, trying to hide her nervousness.

"Can I please go to the restroom?" one of the girls asked. Linda was struck by her courtesy and felt that perhaps things were settling down.

"Of course, but come right back," she said.

"Me too?" another girl chimed in. Linda hesitated. "Please, I really have to go!"

"I am sorry, one at a time."

"But Mrs. Keating lets us go whenever we want, as long as we are back in 5 minutes," the girl pleaded.

"Well, I am not Mrs. Keating," Linda said, glaring at the girl. She glanced at the clock in desperation and began walking around the room, remembering that somebody had suggested that as a method of maintaining class discipline. Her mind began to race. She thought, "Why don't these kids like me?"

Quadrant 1:

Interpersonal Functions

1A:

1B:

1C:

1D:

Quadrant 1:

Interpersonal Functions

1A: Rapidly establishing an appropriate level of rapport with students

1B:

1C:

1D:

Quadrant 1:

Interpersonal Functions

1A: RAPPORT

1B: Establishing and maintaining student discipline in an environment conducive to teaching and learning

1C:

1D:

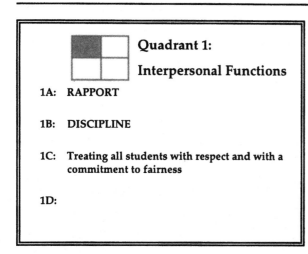

Quadrant 1:

Interpersonal Functions

1A: RAPPORT

1B: DISCIPLINE

1C: Treating all students with respect and with a commitment to fairness

1D:

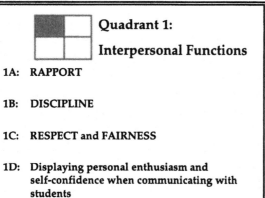

Quadrant 1:

Interpersonal Functions

1A: RAPPORT

1B: DISCIPLINE

1C: RESPECT and FAIRNESS

1D: Displaying personal enthusiasm and self-confidence when communicating with students

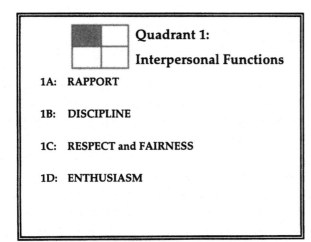

Quadrant 1:

Interpersonal Functions

1A: RAPPORT

1B: DISCIPLINE

1C: RESPECT and FAIRNESS

1D: ENTHUSIASM

Criterion 1A

1A: Rapidly establishing an appropriate level of rapport with students

Criterion 1C

1C: Treating all students with respect and with a commitment to fairness

Instructions

Working in your group, identify five ways in which substitute teaching is like "going on a blind date."

It's Like a Blind Date . . .

Starting a career in substitute teaching is a little bit like going on a blind date.

- Barbara Pronin, 1983, p. 65

5:57

The Importance of Building Rapport and Showing Respect for Students

Maslow's Dichotomy

Maslow's Dichotomy

Psychopathologic

_____

Maslow's Dichotomy

Psychopathologic

_____

Psychotherapeutic

Psychopathologic Defined

Every time you threaten someone or humiliate or hurt unnecessarily or dominate or reject another human being, you become a force for the creation of psychopathology.

- Maslow, 1954, p. 321

Psychotherapeutic Defined

Every time you are kind, helpful, decent, democratic, affectionate, and warm you become a psychotherapeutic force.

- Maslow, 1954, p. 321

Therapies

Therapies

1. LISTEN

Therapies

1. Listen
2. ACCEPT

Therapies

1. Listen
2. Accept
3. RESPECT

Therapies

1. Listen
2. Accept
3. Respect
4. ENCOURAGE

Therapies

1. Listen
2. Accept
3. Respect
4. Encourage
5. PRAISE

Pathogens

Pathogens

1. OVERCOERCIVENESS

Pathogens

1. Overcoerciveness

2. LACK of CONSISTENCY

Pathogens

1. Overcoerciveness

2. Lack of consistency

3. REJECTION

Pathogens

1. Overcoerciveness

2. Lack of consistency

3. Rejection

4. NEGATIVE EXPECTATIONS

Pathogens

1. Overcoerciveness

2. Lack of consistency

3. Rejection

4. Negative expectations

5. CRITICALITY

Pathogens Kill Rapport

5:30

Veteran Substitutes Talk About
Building Rapport

5 Ways to Build Rapport With Students

- Exude enthusiasm for the job.
- Celebrate student diversity.
- Express interest in the students' world.
- Employ student ideas and suggestions.
- Negotiate contracts with students.

5 MORE Ways to Build Rapport With Students

- Model curiosity and wonder.
- Communicate high expectations for all.
- Take instructional risks in the interest of engaging instruction.
- Encourage and praise students.
- Be a caring and interesting person!!!!!

2:30

More Tips on Building Rapport

4 Keys to Successful Subbing

> › Be Yourself
>
> › Be Positive
>
> › Be Honest
>
> › Be Flexible

- Barbara Pronin, 1983, p. 74

"It is you who will set the tone for the day, and you will do it the very first few minutes."

- Barbara Pronin, 1983, p. 66

Information on the Developmental Needs and Characteristics of Students in Different Grade Levels

Overview

Critical to building appropriate rapport with students is having a basic understanding of how children and youth are developmentally different at various ages and grade levels. If you have raised children of your own, or have worked with them in some other capacity, you are aware of how children change dramatically over time. Knowing what specific feelings, behaviors, and attitudes are characteristic of students at various grade levels can help you more effectively communicate respect and fairness and increase your chances of successfully managing student behavior.

Before providing specific information on students at four different grade levels, here are three generic characteristics of students at all grade levels:

1. Students are likely to be most responsive to adults who communicate self-confidence, but who also reveal themselves as fallible human beings.

2. Students are generally respectful of adults they believe accept them for who they are, including their thoughts, beliefs, and opinions.

3. Students at any grade level, when they feel threatened, may choose to retreat from or attack the perceived threat.

As you experience students at different grade levels, you will likely find yourself feeling more comfortable and self-assured when working with particular grade or age groups. This is a very normal and sometimes surprising phenomenon as you discover you enjoy a grade level that you would not have predicted. By reflecting on the information that follows, you increase the possibility that you can find success and enjoyment at any grade level.

I. The Primary Grades (K-2)

1. Children in this age group tend to be eager to please and will frequently do what you ask. Being positive and using praise will generally win students' cooperation. For example, "I like the way that Sarah is lining up for recess."

2. Primary-level children typically have strong developmental needs for activity and social interaction. They also have a limited attention span. Adjust your teaching to short lessons (15-20 minutes) and permit children to move away from their desks periodically throughout the day. Allow for quiet talk, and encourage student participation in the lessons you are teaching.

3. Remember that most children in this age group are not able to read and write fluently. Adjust your expectations so that children are able to be successful by answering questions orally.

4. Children at this age move slowly in completing some psychomotor tasks. Shoes may be slow to be tied, zippers slow to be zipped, and so on. So, when you need to get your class somewhere, allow extra time to meet this developmental need.

5. Kindergarten to second-grade students can be very sensitive about multiple issues including fears about weather (thunder in particular), disagreements with friends, and forgetting their schoolwork.

6. Be patient, sensitive, and creative with this age group. Encourage and support their developing independence. Allow them, as much as possible, to do for themselves.

7. Attempt to keep your schedule as close to the normal routine as possible. This age group notices and responds to change and will be quick to tell you, "We did not do our morning news this morning."

8. Remember how young these children are. Students this age love a good storyteller or book. Reading to them consequently offers you an excellent way to connect with them emotionally.

II. The Lower Grades (3-5)

1. Most children in this age group can read and write, even though there may be wide variations in their abilities. Students will be sensitive about their abilities, so do not call public attention to their mistakes. They will quickly lose interest if discouraged or unable to perform an assignment.

2. Children in Grades 3 to 5 can be depended upon to answer questions you may have about classroom procedures, trips to the office, and other classroom routines. Still sensitive to changes in routine, they may inform you that Ms. Kramer (the regular teacher) "doesn't do it that way."

3. At these grade levels, most students work well in small groups and enjoy the structured time to interact with their peers.

4. This age group is sensitive to criticism, especially any form of public criticism. Speak to children quietly and individually if you have concerns about their behavior.

5. You can be somewhat flexible with your use of instructional time and prolong a class session if warranted by student involvement. For example, these students often love a good discussion.

6. They *generally* are well behaved, respect authority, and follow the rules. Smile and use positive reinforcement throughout the day, as this age group enjoys adult attention and still wants to please them.

7. Treat these children as young learners, but not young children. They do not like being "talked down to."

8. Answer honestly but simply the questions these children ask of you.

9. Whenever possible, use the students' names. Consider using name cards or name tags, as a "name" makes a relationship that is immediate and positive.

10. Attempt to make your directions for lessons as clear and simple as possible. "Confusion" is one of the easiest ways to lose control.

11. Even though they look and act older, they still enjoy being read to, brain teasers, puzzles, and art activities. Consider having some of these activities with you to pull out in the course of a school day in Grades 3 to 5.

III. The Upper Grades (6-8)

1. Students in Grades 6 to 8 often experience some of the greatest physical growth of their childhood years. The rate of growth, however, is uneven. You will see a wide variety of heights and weights in both girls and boys. You may see an awkwardness in physical movement because of these differences. These students are often self-conscious about their physical changes.

2. Maturity levels vary considerably with children in this age group. Often there will be teasing between the boys and the girls. They can have changeable moods and can be uncooperative. Use a sense of humor and avoid being negative.

3. This age group is very conscious of the opinions of their peers. Some students may want to impress their friends rather than be cooperative for a substitute teacher. They have a strong desire to "belong."

4. Be clear, firm, and consistent with your expectations for behavior. They know that they need to cooperate, and they will feel safer in a room where the adult is in charge.

5. Encourage small-group activities. Feel free to assign specific roles and tasks so they know they are accountable. Allow them to periodically move away from their desks to get academic information or interact with each other, as it meets their need for physical movement.

6. Children in Grades 6 to 8 can be quite opinionated. Structure discussions for them to share their thoughts, but be prepared to ensure that interactions are respectful.

7. These students still enjoy having a book read to them. Be sure, however, to have their attention before you begin. If you are on a short-term teaching assignment, read a high-quality picture book for older students. If you are on a long-term assignment, read a chapter from a novel for this age group. The school librarian can help you select quality literature that works well with students in this age group.

8. Be as academically prepared as you can for the different subjects you teach. This will enable you to respond confidently to students' questions. Remember, however, that you do not need to know it all. These students respond positively to a teacher who models being an enthusiastic learner.

IV. High School (9-12)

1. Significant physical growth is also characteristic of students in Grades 9 to 12. These young people are also beginning to mature sexually. They tend to be very conscious of their physical size and attributes. It is important that you project an accepting attitude, making sure to avoid any comments that draw attention to physical characteristics.

2. High-school-age students are experimenting with their adult selves as they transition from adolescence to adulthood. In one respect, they are developmentally similar to toddlers in that they want to be dependent and independent at the same time. Make special efforts to communicate respect for their points of view. Treat them like adults, and they often will respond in an adult manner. Treat them like children, and they often will respond in a childish manner.

3. You may encounter a "know-it-all" attitude from some students who want to challenge your knowledge. Respond with the understanding that this behavior is a developmental issue and not intended as a personal affront. Avoid public confrontations or debates with such students, as this is often their goal.

4. Differences in academic motivation are particularly noticeable in this age group. Be prepared to encounter self-motivated and highly committed students who take school very seriously. Also know that you will experience other students at the opposite end of the continuum, often in the same classroom. Treat students from both groups respectfully.

5. Secondary content is highly specialized. If you find yourself assigned to teach subject matter you do not know, inform students that you don't "speak French" and proceed to help them in the ways suggested by the teacher. Despite your lack of subject-matter expertise, you still can have a positive influence.

6. You can project a sense of respect for these students by creating an accepting classroom environment. Be willing to negotiate with these students so that they feel you are sensitive to their personal and academic needs.

7. Despite their posturing, most students in this age group want to have an adult that is in charge of the classroom. Know the classroom rules and be fair and consistent in interacting with the students.

Module 5

Bringing Your "Self" to
School

Criterion 1D

1D: Displaying personal
enthusiasm and self-
confidence when
communicating with
students

Self-Disclosure: revealing how
one is reacting to a present situation
and giving any information about one's
past that is relevant to an understanding
of one's reaction to the present.

- David Johnson, 1993, p. 30

:40

**Veteran Substitutes Talk About
Sharing Life Experiences**

Appropriate Self-Disclosure

Example: Students in a 10th-grade math class share their frustration about an unpopular school policy.

Appropriate Self-Disclosure

Example: Students in a 10th-grade math class share their frustration about an unpopular school policy. **The substitute teacher shares a story about a similar situation when she was in high school.**

Less-Appropriate Self-Disclosure

Example: A substitute teacher introduces himself to a 7th-grade class he has never met before . . .

Less-Appropriate Self-Disclosure

Example: A substitute teacher introduces himself to a 7th-grade class he has never met before **by telling them about the rock concert he attended the previous night.**

Content-Connected Self-Disclosure

Example: A 4th-grade class is studying the solar system in science.

Content-Connected Self-Disclosure

Example: A 4th-grade class is studying the solar system in science. **The substitute teacher tells the class about his hobby of astronomy and what he hopes to see with his new telescope.**

Content-Connected Self-Disclosure

Example: An 8th-grade American history class is discussing the civil rights movement.

Content-Connected Self-Disclosure

Example: An 8th-grade American history class is discussing the civil rights movement. **The substitute teacher shares her experience as a college student when she went to Alabama to help register black voters.**

Content-Connected Self-Disclosure

Example: A Spanish IV class is studying Spanish literature.

Content-Connected Self-Disclosure

Example: A Spanish IV class is studying Spanish literature. **The sub describes his interest in bullfighting and asks students questions about bullfighting in Spanish literature.**

Instructions

Working alone, for each of the following situations quickly make a note as to a "content-connected" self-disclosure you might make. No discussion, please.

Connecting Yourself to Content

Content	My Content-Connected Self-Disclosure
An 8th-grade history class is studying World War II. I would . . .	
A 3rd-grade class is studying the water cycle. I would . . .	
A 12th-grade American literature class is reading and discussing *The Scarlet Letter*. I would . . .	
A 1st-grade class is hatching baby chicks for a science project. I would . . .	
A 5th-grade class is studying geometric shapes in the environment. I would . . .	
A 10th-grade health class is studying the use of chemicals in food. I would . . .	

Content-Connected Self-Disclosure

An 8th-grade history class is studying World War II.

The substitute teacher . . .

Content-Connected Self-Disclosure

A 3rd-grade class is studying the water cycle.

The substitute teacher . . .

Content-Connected Self-Disclosure

A 12th-grade American literature class is reading and discussing *The Scarlet Letter*.

The substitute teacher . . .

A

Content-Connected Self-Disclosure

A 1st-grade class is hatching baby chicks for a science project.

The substitute teacher . . .

Content-Connected Self-Disclosure

A 5th-grade class is studying geometric shapes in the environment.

The substitute teacher . . .

Content-Connected Self-Disclosure

A 10th-grade health class is studying the use of chemicals in food.

The substitute teacher . . .

Processing your

_____

Ideas on how to connect to content

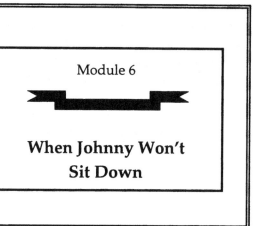

Module 6

When Johnny Won't
Sit Down

**Quadrant 1:
Interpersonal Functions**

- 1A: Rapport
- 1B: Establishing and maintaining student discipline in an environment conducive to teaching and learning
- 1C: Respect and fairness
- 1D: Enthusiasm and confidence

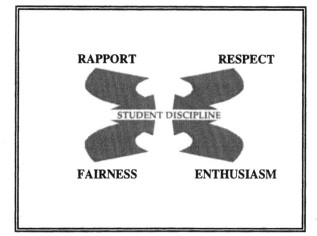

RAPPORT   **RESPECT**

STUDENT DISCIPLINE

FAIRNESS   **ENTHUSIASM**

Criterion 1B

1B: Establishing and maintaining student discipline in an environment conducive to teaching and learning

---

"People had been talking about it all through lunch, thinking of things they wanted to do, remembering stuff their brothers and sisters and even parents had told them they'd done. So when we got to the room, everyone's plans started rolling right away . . ."

- Jamie Gilson, 1982, p. 59

3:30

Tricks Students Play on Substitutes

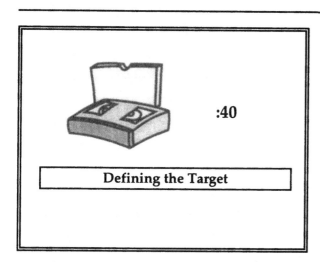

:40

Defining the Target

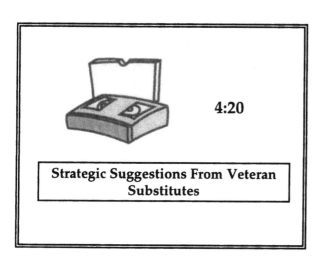

4:20

**Strategic Suggestions From Veteran
Substitutes**

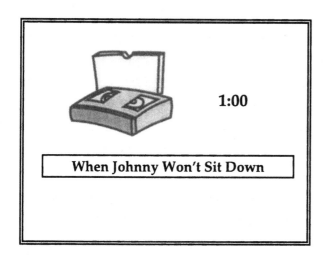

1:00

When Johnny Won't Sit Down

Instructions

1. Working in your group, record five possible strategies for responding to the student who won't sit down.

Instructions

2. Make notes on the ideas from veteran substitutes on what to do about the student who won't sit down.

4:20

Veteran Substitutes' Responses

Instructions

3. Compare and contrast your responses with those of the veteran substitutes.

Managing Student Behavior

Advice from:

Aurelia, Denise, Marlene, and Mike

Recognize that you ARE in a position of authority.

- Mike

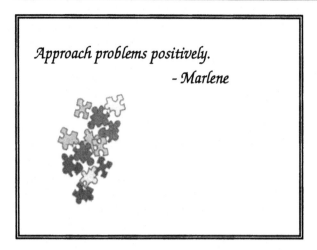

Approach problems positively.
                    - Marlene

Explore the causes.
                    - Aurelia

Provide warnings and a second chance.
                    - Denise

Employ private conferences.
                    - Mike

Change instruction.
        - Denise

Use "time-out."
                    - Mike

Deny privileges.
- Marlene

Disciplinary *DO's*

- Clearly state your rules early.
- Respect the school's and teacher's rules.
- Communicate positive expectations.
- Treat deviant behavior unemotionally.
- Employ appropriate rewards.
- Provide warnings.
- Follow through with consistency.

Disciplinary *DO NOTs*

- ▼ Nag and scold
- ▼ Threaten or humiliate
- ▼ Issue ultimatums
- ▼ Overreact
- ▼ Make arbitrary judgments
- ▼ Yell or scream
- ▼ Employ harsh or unusual punishment

Module 6: When Johnny Won't Sit Down

"Class," (the sub) announced, "I have found Mr. Star's lesson plans . . . and you are to do pages 89 and 90 in your math book. I suggest you start on them right now." She waited, and when none of the talking stopped, added, "Or else." "Or else what?" Rolf asked. And we all listened for the answer.

 - Jamie Gilson, 1982, p. 65

2:00

Power Play Dynamics

3:45

Discipline Advice From Veteran Teachers

Module 7

Managing Student Behavior

Instructions

Complete and then score the *Student Discipline Inventory*.

Three Approaches to Managing Student Behavior

- **Intervention**

- **Nonintervention**

- **Interaction**

- Glickman and Tamashiro, 1980

Student Discipline Inventory

INSTRUCTIONS: For each question below, there are two statements, A and B. Choose the statement that is closest to how you feel. You might not agree with either choice, but you must choose one. Circle either A or B, but not both. Please be sure to answer all 12 items.

1. A. Students are not always capable of making rational and moral decisions.
    B. Students' inner emotions and capacity for decision making must always be considered legitimate and valid.

2. A. If I were a full-time classroom teacher, I would assign students to specific areas or seats in the classroom.
    B. If I were a full-time classroom teacher, my seating (or work area) assignments would be open to negotiation.

3. A. Even though students are not fully mature, teachers should give them responsibility and choices.
    B. Students should not be expected to be fully responsible for their decisions because they are strongly influenced by teachers, parents, friends, and TV.

4. When the noise level in the classroom bothers me, I will most likely:
    A. Discuss my discomfort with the students and attempt to come to a compromise with them about noise levels during activity periods.
    B. Allow the activity to continue as long as the noise is not disturbing or upsetting any student.

5. During class, if a student breaks a classmate's portable CD player, I as a teacher will most likely:
    A. Scold both students, one for disrespecting the other's property and the other for breaking a rule prohibiting personal radios and CD players in school.
    B. Avoid interfering in something that the students (and possibly their parents) need to resolve themselves.

6. If students unanimously agree that a classroom rule is unjust and should be removed, but I (the teacher) disagree with them, then:
    A. The rule should probably be removed and replaced by a rule made by the students.
    B. The students and I should jointly decide on a fair rule.

7. When a student does not join in a group activity:
    A. The teacher should explain the value of the activity to the student and encourage the student to participate.
    B. The teacher should attempt to identify the student's reason for not joining and create activities that meet the needs of the student.

8. During the first few minutes of class, I will most likely:
    A. Allow the students to inform me of what rules are in place in the classroom.
    B. Announce the classroom rules as I understand them and inform students that the rules will be fairly enforced.

9. A. Students' creativity and self-expression should be encouraged and nurtured as much as possible.
    B. Limits on distracting behaviors have to be set without denying students their sense of choice.

10. If a student interrupts my lesson by talking to a neighbor, I will most likely:
    A. Move the child away from other students and continue the lesson. Class time should not be wasted because of the behavior of one student.
    B. Tell students about my annoyance and conduct a discussion with students about how they feel when being interrupted.

11. A. A good educator is firm but fair in disciplining violators of school rules.
    B. A good educator discusses several alternative disciplinary actions with a student who violates a school rule.

12. When one of the more conscientious students does not complete an assignment on time:
    A. I know the student has a legitimate reason, and know the student will turn in the assignment on his or her own.
    B. I tell the student that he or she was expected to turn in the assignment when it was due, and then the student and I will jointly decide on the next steps.

Source: Glickman, C.D., & Tamashiro, R.T. (1980). "Clarifying Teachers' Beliefs About Discipline." *Educational Leadership, 37*(6), 459-465. Reprinted with permission from ASCD. All rights reserved.

Scoring the Inventory

Step 1. Circle your responses on the following table and then tally the totals in each table.

Table 1		Table 2		Table 3	
1A	2A	1B	4B	2B	4A
3B	5A	5B	6A	3A	6B
7A	8B	8A	9A	7B	9B
10A	11A	10B	12A	11B	12B

Step 2. Multiply the totals from each table above by 8.33.

2.1 Total responses in Table 1 _____ x 8.33 = _____

2.2 Total responses in Table 2 _____ x 8.33 = _____

2.3 Total responses in Table 3 _____ x 8.33 = _____

Step 3. Before interpreting your results, check to see that the sum of your responses in Table 1, Table 2, and Table 3 equals 12.

The product that you obtained in Step 2.1 above is an approximate percentage of how often you would likely take an *interventionist* approach to discipline, rather than either a noninterventionist or interactionalist approach.

The product you obtained in Step 2.2 above is an approximate percentage of how often you would likely take a *noninterventionist* approach to discipline, rather than one of the other approaches.

The product you obtained in Step 2.3 is an approximate percentage of how often you would likely take an *interactionalist* approach to discipline, rather than one of the other approaches.

By comparing the three percentage values computed in Step 2 above (2.1, 2.2, 2.3) you can assess which discipline model you tend to favor. If the percentage values are equal, or close to equal, you may be eclectic in your approach.

Note: Items 2 and 8 are adjusted to reflect a substitute teaching context.
Source: Glickman, C.D., & Tamashiro, R.T. (1980). "Clarifying Teachers' Beliefs About Discipline." *Educational Leadership, 37*(6), 459-465. Reprinted with permission from ASCD. All rights reserved.

When to Use Intervention

When the age or maturity level of the students is LOW, OR . . .

When to Use Intervention

Working as a whole group, quickly brainstorm five reasons why you might choose to employ intervention.

When to Use Intervention

⇨ When student wellness is at risk
⇨ When your authority must be validated
⇨ When your intentions must be made clear
⇨ When other professionals are needed
⇨ When other strategies are ineffective

When to Use Interaction

When the age or maturity level of the students is MODERATE

OR . . .

When to Use Interaction

Working as a whole group, quickly brainstorm five reasons why you might choose to employ interaction.

When to Use Interaction

⇨ When attention or recognition may be helpful
⇨ When relationship building is important
⇨ When information is needed
⇨ When you want to avoid public confrontation
⇨ When other strategies are ineffective

When to Use Nonintervention

When the age or maturity
level of the students is HIGH,
OR . . .

When to Use Nonintervention

Working as a whole group, quickly
brainstorm five reasons why you might
choose to employ nonintervention.

When to Use Nonintervention

⇨ When you want students to practice self-control
⇨ When the misbehavior is minor or temporary
⇨ When the offender is seeking teacher attention
⇨ When you want to communicate tolerance
⇨ When you choose to allow peer pressure to work
⇨ When other strategies are ineffective

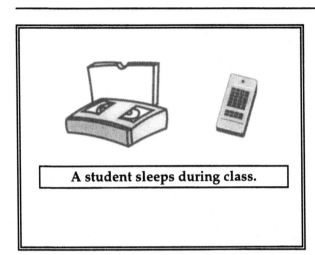

A student sleeps during class.

Teacher meets with student after class.

Student talks back to the teacher who then issues a reprimand.

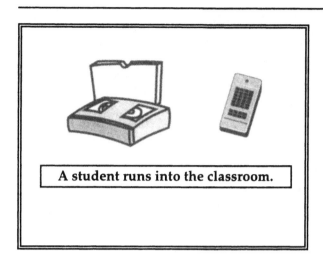

A student runs into the classroom.

A student rocks chair during seatwork.

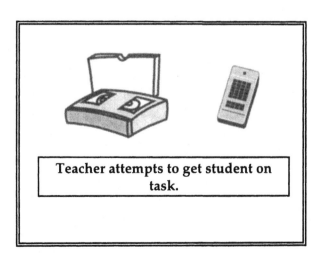

Teacher attempts to get student on task.

Teacher calls on disinterested student.

Teacher calls on disinterested student.

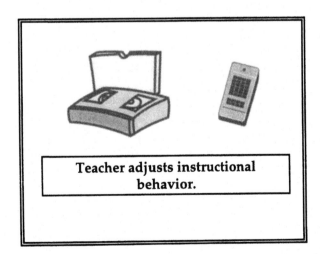

Teacher adjusts instructional behavior.

Module 7: Managing Student Behavior

Teacher ignores student chatter.

Teacher conferences with student who has been in a playground fight.

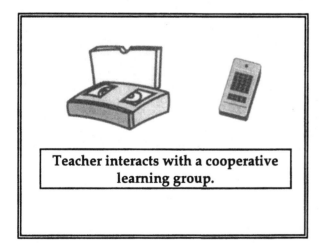

Teacher interacts with a cooperative learning group.

A CHECKLIST ON DISCIPLINE FOR SUBSTITUTE TEACHERS

	Usually	Sometimes	Never
1. I get students' attention before giving instruction(s).			
2. I wait for students to attend rather than talk over chatter.			
3. I quickly get students on task.			
4. I give clear and specific instructions.			
5. I set explicit time limits for task completion.			
6. I circulate among students at work.			
7. I hold private conferences/conversations during class.			
8. I model courtesy and politeness.			
9. I use a quiet voice in the classroom.			
10. I use the "soft reprimand" rather than raise my voice.			
11. I use a variety of cues to remind students of expected behavior.			
12. I teach students my cues for gaining their attention.			
13. I am aware of the effects of my dress, voice, and movements on the students' behavior.			
14. I use students' names as low-profile correctors of inattention.			
15. I use proximity to improve classroom control.			
16. I communicate positive expectations of good behavior to students.			
17. I am aware of school and classroom rules.			
18. I refuse to threaten or plead with students.			
19. I consistently follow through with consequences to enforce rules.			
20. I respond to behaviors I like with specific, personal praise.			
21. I use nonverbal, social, and activity reinforcers.			

☆Shooting for the Stars☆

A Positive Approach to Student Discipline in the Elementary Grades

INSTRUCTIONS: Before students arrive, draw three stars on the board. After explaining the classroom rules for the day, reveal the meaning of the three stars in this way:

"Each star represents 5 minutes of bonus recess to be give to the class at the end of the day. There are three stars, so you have already earned 15 minutes of extra recess at the end of the day. This is a gift from me to you.

I think you are a three-star class, but you have to prove it to me by following the rules of good behavior today. You need to get quiet when I ask you, walk quietly down the hall, and treat everyone with respect.

If you don't do these things, I will give you a warning, If you still don't follow the rules, I will erase a star. Once a star is gone, it is gone forever.

If you keep all three stars on the board and get your work done, we will have 15 minutes of extra recess at the end of the day and I will leave a note telling your teacher that you were an EXCELLENT CLASS.

If you have two stars left at the end of the day, we will have 10 minutes of extra recess and I will tell your teacher that you were a GOOD CLASS.

If you have one star left, we will have 5 minutes of extra recess inside the classroom and I will tell your teacher that you were a PRETTY GOOD CLASS.

If there are no stars left, I will let your teacher know that you had trouble behaving today. She won't want to hear that, will she?

So, you see, it is up to you what kind of report I leave your teacher, and how much extra recess you get today. Do your best, and let's keep those stars up there."

Source: Sue A. Chaney, 1995.

Module 8

Just What the Teacher
Ordered

**Quadrant 2:
Instructional Functions**

- **2A:** Clearly articulating the goals and procedures of the lesson to be taught
- **2B:** Making efficient and meaningful use of instructional time
- **2C:** Interpreting, implementing, and enhancing instructional plans prescribed by the regular teacher
- **2D:** Employing instructional techniques designed to assess students prior knowledge and extend students' thinking

Criterion 2C

2C: Interpreting, implementing, and enhancing instructional plans prescribed by the regular teacher

Instructions

Working in your group, take 10 minutes to discuss the sample lesson plans.

Using the plans as specific examples, construct three *general questions* regarding lesson plans and substitute teaching.

1:30

**Following Lesson Plans:
The Administrative Perspective**

2:30

**Following Lesson Plans:
The Teacher Perspective**

1:00

Following Lesson Plans:
The Substitute Perspective

Behavioral Objective:

An instructional outcome expressed in terms of a desired student behavior in the cognitive, affective, or psychomotor domains

---

TSWBAT

The student will be able to . . .

For example . . .

Workshop participants will be able to interpret an instructional plan in terms of the desired behavioral outcome.

Bloom's Taxonomy

A conceptual framework for organizing the cognitive levels of human thought

Bloom's Taxonomy Levels

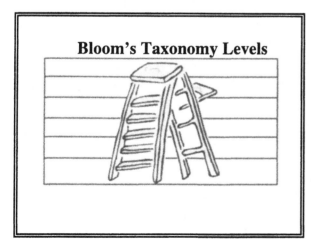

Bloom's Taxonomy Levels

♦	Evaluation
♦	Synthesis
♦	Analysis
♦	Application
♦	Comprehension
♦ Knowledge	

Behavioral Verbs are *instructional building blocks!*

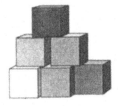

Behavioral Verbs are *instructional building blocks!*

Behavioral Verbs are *instructional building blocks!*

Behavioral Verbs are *instructional building blocks!*

Behavioral Verbs for

Knowledge	Comprehension	Application

Behavioral Verbs for

Knowledge	Comprehension	Application
Find	Discuss*	Choose
Identify	Explain*	Demonstrate
Label*	Illustrate	Produce*
Name	Locate	Select*
Recite	Summarize	
Transfer		

Behavioral Verbs for

Analysis	Synthesis	Evaluation
Compare*	Construct	Choose
Contrast*	Create*	Decide*
Diagram	Develop	Judge
Examine*	Integrate*	Prioritize
Research	Produce	Select

Instructions

Working in your group, take 5 minutes to complete the sample lesson plan worksheet.

Lesson Plan Worksheet

Now that you are familiar with Bloom's Taxonomy, refer to the lesson plans on pages 81-86 of your notebook. Complete the following chart, identifying in each lesson plan one or more behavioral verbs that are used and their related level on Bloom's Taxonomy. The behavioral verb chart on page 80 will help you complete this task.

Lesson Plan	Behavioral Verbs	Level on Bloom's Taxonomy
Ms. Janet McIntyre 1st Grade Math		
Mr. Bill Martin 4th Grade Language Arts		
Ms. Miller 6th Grade Daily Plan		
Mr. Michael Allen 12th Grade Biology II		

Examples of Verbs to Use in Objective Writing

Knowledge	Comprehension	Application	Analysis	Synthesis	Evaluation
Arrange	Account for	Adopt	Break down	Blend	Accept
Choose	Alter	Apply	Canvass	Build	Appraise
Cite	Calculate	Capitalize	Check	Cause	Arbitrate
Define	Change	Collect	Deduce	Combine	Assess
Group	Comprehend	Construct	Diagram	Compile	Award
Identify	Convert	Employ	Dissect	Compose	Censure
Label	Define	Exercise	Divide	Conceive	Classify
List	Expand	Handle	Examine	Create	Conclude
Locate	Explain	Make use of	Include	Design	Criticize
Match	Interpret	Manipulate	Infer	Develop	Decide
Outline	Project	Operate	Inspect	Evolve	Describe
Pick	Propose	Put to use	Look into	Formulate	Determine
Quote	Qualify	Relate	Reason	Make	Discriminate
Recite	Spell out	Solve	Screen	Modify	Grade
Repeat	Submit	Try	Search	Produce	Interpret
Reproduce	Transform	Use	Section	Rearrange	Judge
Say		Utilize	Separate	Reconstruct	Justify
Show		Wield	Sift	Reorganize	Prioritize
Spell			Study	Revise	Rank
Tally			Survey	Structure	Rate
Tell			Take apart	Yield	Reject
Write			Test for		Settle
			Uncover		Summarize
					Support
					Weigh

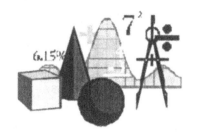 

**From the desk of
Ms. Janet McIntyre
Kennedy Elementary
First Grade
February 2**

Math Lesson :

Twenty-five baggies of assorted items are under my desk. The children should explain common relationships of items by sorting them into groups by some common attribute.

1. Pass out a baggy to each child.

2. Have each child work with a partner.

3. They should first sort their items.

4. After they are both finished, they should explain to their partner what the common attribute is.

5. Walk around the class with the checklist hanging on the wall behind my desk. Please note whether each child can sort their items and explain the common attribute.

Welcome to Our Room

Mr. Bill Martin
South Elementary
April 7

Good morning and welcome to our room. Thanks for being here today while I am out at the Children's Literature Conference. My children are all very helpful, and I don't think you will have any problems. Attached you will find the lesson plans for language arts. The plans for science, social studies, etc. are next to my plan book.

9:00 - 10:30 a.m. All of the children are working from a variety of Children's Literature in the classroom on the topic of our community, Ridgewood. This is the third week in a 4-week unit. All of the children have the necessary paper, pencils, and other supplies needed. They should each have a chart that has the squares differentiated for:

      Ridgewood Today

      Ridgewood in the Past

Please ask Amber (who is the "Child of the Week") if you have any questions.

Objective: The children will be organizing and writing their information from their interviews of an elder community member into the form stated above. They should specifically be working on the "Ridgewood in the Past" squares today.

Procedures:

1. This is the first lesson of the day after lunch count, attendance, etc. so the children will be a little noisy.

2. Begin the lesson by reading from the picture book *Who Came Down That Road*? by George Ella Lyon. It is on the top of my desk.

3. Read slowly and feel free to have the children respond spontaneously, but do not allow the responses to go on for too long as you will lose most children's attention. (The children can stay at their desks, but they are free to color quietly or put their heads down while you read, as long as they are not disrupting you or the other children.)

4. After completing the book (allow about 15 minutes), ask them the following questions:

    a. What was this story about?
    b. Describe the illustrations in the book.
    c. What special words did the author use that helped you hear or see things in the book?
    d. Why was this book chosen for today's lesson?

(Again, allow about 10 minutes for this discussion, and do not allow children to talk too much.)

5. Transition to their activity by asking the children if the person they interviewed from Ridgewood "came down the same road" that they have walked? Ask them to explain their answers to see if they understood the connection. (Some will probably understand, others may not.)

6. Ask them to get out their "Ridgewood" charts. (They will know what this is.) Ask them to get out their outline of their interview with their community member. They have already filled out the left-column of the categories that they chose to create their compare-and-contrast chart of Ridgewood "Today" and "In The Past." (Most of the children have the same categories, but those were decided upon by their interview. For example, they may be stores, houses, schools, etc.)

7. Allow them about 40 minutes to work on their charts. They will work fairly independently but may ask for help with spelling, wording, etc. Encourage them to think about how the word begins and to use the dictionary. (There are about 10 primary ones on the back shelf --- they will know where they are.) Remember, we have been working on this unit for 3 weeks, so they are familiar with all the resources in the classroom.

8. If everything has gone as planned, you have about 15 minutes left in the lesson. The children must be ready to go to Computers at 10:30, so be mindful of the time. Ask individual children to come up to the stool at the front of the room and share what they have written on their charts so far. This can serve as a reminder to children who perhaps are not constructing their charts properly. Allow the children in the class to ask questions of the children sharing. Ensure that the children are listening carefully with respect to their peers. You may want to walk the classroom during this whole lesson to be available for assistance. They are seated in groups of four and are allowed to talk quietly with each other so they may easily solve their own problems.

Evaluation: Because this is one day's work on an activity that involves many days' work, I will be able to see the progress on the chart when I return. But the overall evaluation is on how well the comparison and contrasting of the information was presented in the chart form. The quality of the work on the form represents the work from the interview and the organization of that interview.

This is a small version of the chart that they already have for this lesson. There are extras in my top desk drawer if you need them.

Ridgewood Today	Ridgewood in the Past

For the Week Beginning: _____ October 12, 1996 _____ Ms. Miller

GRADE SUBJECT	GRADE SUBJECT	GRADE SUBJECT
9:30 to 11:00	Ask children to read pages 73-75 silently. Ask ?'s about Oregon Trail (pg. 75)	History Series The American West (pgs. 73-75) (Objective 3.5)
11:00 to 12:00	Lunch	
12:00 to 1:00	Art	
1:00 to 1:25	Recess	Duty
1:25 to 2:00	Read aloud up to go	and pack home.

Mr. Michael Allen
Lesson: <u>SUCCESSION</u>

Grades: 11 and 12
Subject: Biology II

LEARNING OUTCOMES

<u>KNOWLEDGE OBJECTIVES</u>:

EBO 1:   To know that the process of progressive change in nature is a constant condition in ecosystems that plays an important role in determining the biological composition of the community (TBO 2)

EBO 2:   To be able to describe the difference between primary and secondary succession by being able to discuss an example of each (TBO 2)

EBO 3:   To know that succession, if altered, culminates in the climax community, and be able to discuss the uniqueness and value of the climax community (TBO 2)

<u>SKILL OBJECTIVES</u>:

EBO 4:   To be able to identify at least four human activities in their local environment which work to retard succession (TBO 4)

<u>AFFECTIVE OBJECTIVES</u>:

EBO 5:   To consider the value conflict surrounding the question of whether preserving a climax forest system is "wasting" valuable natural resources (TBO 4) (GS 6)

LEARNING MATERIALS

LM 1:   Reading 6, Chapter 1, *A Human Ecology Primer*

LM 2:   Overheads illustrating the several stages in the succession of 1) a deciduous forest, and 2) an alpine lake.

LEARNING MATERIALS

LA 1:   Discuss the concept of succession using local environments to illustrate (e.g., the Beech-Maple climax forest at Hueston Woods State Park).

LA 2:   Show overheads and discuss aquatic succession.

LA 3:   Discuss the value of the climax community and how human intervention has made such communities scarce resources.

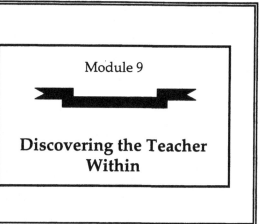

Module 9

Discovering the Teacher Within

Criterion 2C

2C: Interpreting, implementing, and enhancing instructional plans prescribed by the regular classroom teacher

Teaching as *Science*

". . . good teaching will someday be attainable by following rigorous laws that yield high predictability and control."

- N. L. Gage, 1978, p. 17

Teaching as *Art*

"As . . . art, teaching must be recognized as a process that calls for intuition, creativity, improvisation, and expressiveness . . ."

- N. L. Gage, 1978, p. 15

3:30

Enhancing the Teacher's Plans

Assignment:

Working with a partner from your group, choose one of the lesson plans you discussed earlier. Together, quickly fashion a way to enhance the plan and still meet the teacher's objectives.

Time: 10 minutes

Share your lesson plan enhancements.

Substitute Teacher Categories

• The Baby-Sitter

• The Bare-Minimum Sub

• The Improviser

- Jackson M. Drake, 1981, p. 130

Module 10

Something From Nothing

Criterion 2A

2A: Clearly articulating the goals and procedures of the lesson to be taught

---

Criterion 2B

2B: Making efficient and meaningful use of instructional time

Case Study #2

Instructions

Read the case and quickly begin thinking about how you might respond in this situation. Be prepared to share your ideas.

2:36

When There Are No Plans

**What to Do
When There Are NO Plans!**

Case Study #2

Michael Campbell was out of work. At age 28, and with 6 years of experience as a graphic artist, he still couldn't believe he had lost his job. Downsizing was something that happened to other people, not him. After a couple weeks of being mildly depressed, Michael decided that perhaps there was a silver lining in this cloud of temporary unemployment. During his college years, Michael had thought seriously about a career in art education. Maybe now was the time to test the waters.

A month later, following a couple of visits to the local university, Michael enrolled in a teacher certification program and obtained a temporary certificate permitting him to begin substitute teaching.

It was the beginning of November, and Michael had been working 2 to 3 days per week in one district or another. He was beginning to get the "feel" of teaching and was increasingly confident about his decision to pursue a new career in education.

Then, early one morning in November, Michael received a call from the secretary at Kennedy Junior High School asking him to substitute for Mrs. Brady, an eighth-grade language arts teacher. Mrs. Brady's husband had been in a serious car accident the night before, and she would not be at school.

Michael proceeded to Kennedy where the mood of the school was quite somber. Mrs. Brady's husband was in intensive care, and many of the staff members were visibly shaken by the news of the accident. Michael quietly proceeded to Mrs. Brady's classroom, feeling a little awkward about the situation. Arriving at Mrs. Brady's desk, he quickly discovered that there were no lesson plans. It was obvious that she had fully intended to be in school the next day and had likely taken her plan book home.

As he sat at the teacher's desk contemplating his next move, he heard the first-period bell and then the sound of student voices in the hall.

What was Michael going to do with the 28 eighth graders who were headed his way?

**What to Do
When There Are NO Plans!**

✔**Talk to team teachers**

**What to Do
When There Are NO Plans!**

✔**See the secretary**

**What to Do
When There Are NO Plans!**

✔**Speak with students**

**What to Do
When There Are NO Plans!**

✔Read the room

**What to Do
When There Are NO Plans!**

✔Employ a back-up plan!

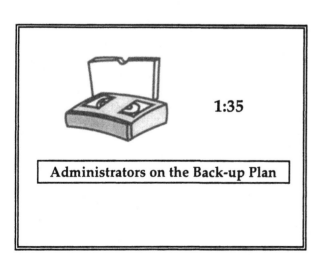

1:35

Administrators on the Back-up Plan

Qualities of the *Ideal* Back-up Plan

* Objective driven
* Personally exciting
* Adaptable to all grade levels
* Capable of generating high student interest
* Hands-on/minds-on activities

Module 11

Getting in Flow

Criterion 2D

2D: Employing instructional techniques designed to assess students' prior knowledge and extend students' thinking

Flow

Theory

-Mihaly Csikszentmihalyi, 1978

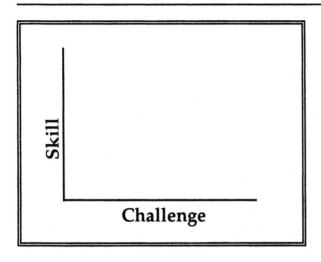

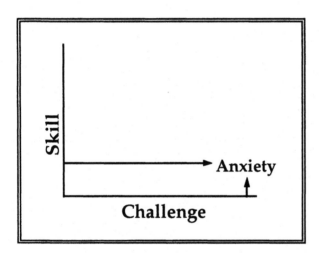

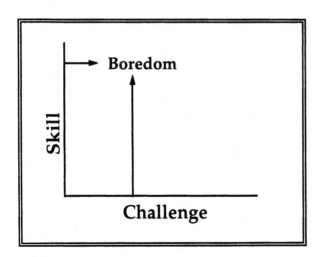

Module 11: Getting in Flow

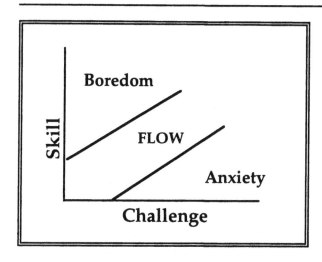

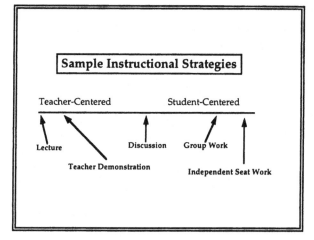

Case Study #3

Instructions

1. Read the case and construct a plan that can help the teacher have a productive day where student learning is not compromised. You may refer to the Student-Centered Instructional Strategies which appears at the end of this Module on page number 100.

2. Select one plan from your small group to share with the whole group.

Case Study #3

After 6 months, she had finally grown accustomed to the early morning phone calls. One of the things that surprised Carmen Carter was how much she enjoyed the variety that substitute teaching afforded. Indeed, every call was an invitation to a new adventure, especially those "middle school calls." Actually, Carmen had to admit that she had come to welcome middle school assignments more than any others. This was quite a turnaround from her initial aversion to working with young adolescents. So, she was more than happy to accept an assignment to Walnut Grove Middle School.

Arriving at the office at Walnut Grove, Carmen was greeted by the school secretary who she knew from previous assignments. "Carmen, there has been a change of plans," said the secretary. "The high school principal called a few minutes ago, and he is desperate for a sub. One of his teachers left unexpectedly after first period and he called Mrs. Jones (middle school principal) to see if she could send a sub his way. You're it. We are going to cover our first two periods with teachers who are on planning period and we have a sub coming in for third. You need to get up to the high school now. "

As a sub, Carmen was getting used to curve balls, but this was something new. Ten minutes later, she was at the counter in the high school office. "I am the sub from the middle school," Carmen explained. "Fantastic," responded the secretary, "You're just in time for third period. You're filling in for Mr. Kellman, the Algebra II teacher." "Algebra II," Carmen said to herself. One of her greatest fears was being realized. Carmen had always found mathematics incomprehensible, and now she was remembering how embarrassed she was when she earned a D by the skin of her teeth in high school algebra.

Momentarily, she thought about backing out and finding some reason to reject the assignment. Then she suddenly remembered the words of her grandfather, who always advised her that the best way to meet a challenge was to take it "head on." Her grandfather's words rang in her ears as she walked the polished marble hallway toward Room 113. How could she teach subject matter that she feared and, to be honest, hated? These questions haunted her as she grew closer to the room and realized that many students were already in the room discussing the fact that they would be having a sub.

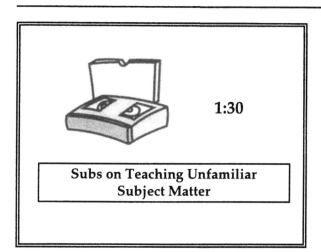

1:30

Subs on Teaching Unfamiliar Subject Matter

Student-Centered Instructional Strategies

The following eight instructional strategies on pages 103-106 can be effective tools for promoting *student-centered learning*. Such strategies place the teacher in the role of facilitator or guide rather than content knowledge expert, making them excellent choices when a substitute teacher is confronted with unfamiliar subject matter, or situations when there are no lesson plans. Such strategies promote student thinking and are effective tools employed by veteran teachers.

Prior to providing a brief explanation of each of the strategies, consider the following important guidelines for facilitating student-centered learning activities:

- First, remember that none of the following activities will be successful if they are presented in a negative or coercive manner. Approach students with an inviting and respectful attitude and you have a fighting chance that they will engage the activity.

- Remember that you must communicate to students that you are interested in their thinking. When students are working in groups, for example, circulate around the room monitoring their performance.

- While monitoring, look for opportunities to encourage or praise students for their efforts. Use specific, public, praise for groups that are on-task and following the instructional procedures.

- Express your own intellectual curiosity by raising questions that communicate your interest in the subject matter being explored. If you do so in a genuine manner, students will usually respond in a positive fashion. In short, model being a learner!

- Whenever possible, collect an artifact from each student that provides evidence of their thinking. Such documents help the regular teacher understand what took place in his or her absence and may provide interesting insights into the students' understanding or misunderstanding of the material.

1. **Expert Panel**. In this student-centered strategy, students elect three to five classmates to serve as experts on the subject matter being studied. To avoid embarrassing students, use a secret ballot approach, asking each student to make three nominations. Collect the ballots and ask a student or two to assist you in doing a quick tally to determine the students' preferences for the panelists.

   Next, ask the nominees to serve on the panel. Invite and encourage the nominees to participate. Do not force students to serve as a panelist if they resist. Once the panel is set, encourage and facilitate the class to ask the expert panel questions about areas of knowledge or skill development they do not clearly understand. Panelists may choose to respond by explaining or demonstrating.

2. **Debate**. This strategy is particularly effective in subjects such as language arts and social studies where interpretation, analysis, and informed judgments are valued processes. After some initial questioning to determine if there are areas of significant disagreement about a particular event, subject, reading, or issue, ask students to take 5 to 10 minutes to draft a personal position statement on the topic.

   Next, divide the class into two camps and serve as a facilitator for the debate. It is important that you (with the students' help) identify three to four rules or procedures that will govern the debate. If the issue does not divide the class equally, ask for a smaller group of volunteers to represent each position and then have the rest of the class process the debate by making notes on the key points made by each side. Consider collecting these papers at the end of the period as evidence of the students' involvement. For an interesting twist, require students to argue the position that opposes their point of view.

3. **Demonstrations or Performances**. Subject matter such as mathematics, writing, speech, and dramatics, to name a few, lend themselves well to physical demonstrations that can be helpful to the participants as well as the observers. One goal of this type of instructional approach is to encourage students to "think about their thinking." Once you have identified a skill that can be demonstrated, ask for volunteers who would be willing to demonstrate that skill for their peers.

   After a demonstration has been completed, facilitate the rest of the class in asking questions of the student who demonstrated or performed. It is important to help students understand that they are not to criticize or judge, but rather to ask questions of the performer that will help clarify their own thinking or the thinking of the performer.

4. **Dyad Interviews**. The purpose of this instructional strategy is to foster dialogue and reflection between two-student teams, or *dyads*. Prior to structuring the dyads, give students 5 to 10 minutes to work independently to construct three to five interview questions they would like to ask a classmate regarding the material they are studying. Depending on the age of the students, you might want to explain that this is a common task that journalists and researchers do as part of their work.

Depending on the subject matter, the questions may be designed to discover how another student feels about a particular reading or film the class has recently studied. In other cases, questions are structured to help the interviewer understand a particular aspect of subject matter that is confusing or challenging. Instruct the students to record the questions on a piece of looseleaf paper that you will collect at the end of the activity.

Next, structure the dyads by allowing students to choose a partner or by employing a random assignment technique. There are advantages to both approaches and you will have to use your judgment regarding which approach to take. Allowing students to choose their partner builds rapport but may lead to off-task behavior as students interact with their friends. This can often be controlled by being clear that you will collect the work. If students complete the activity early, the remaining class time can be used for quiet study.

After the dyads are set, allow 6 to 8 minutes for the first round of interviews. Instruct the interviewers that they are to take notes on the same paper on which they wrote their questions. When time is up, reverse the roles, and allow another 8 minutes for the second round of interviews. Next, ask students to return to their regular seats and answer the following question in writing: What did you learn from your interview? Give the students approximately 7 to 10 minutes to record their response on the same piece of paper they have been using. Instruct the students that their responses should not contain the name of the person they interviewed.

5. **Team Competition**. This approach to student-centered instruction can take many forms that often follow the formats of popular TV game shows or traditional parlor games. Full-time teachers often use such academic competitions to review for an upcoming quiz or test. The number of variations and enhancements are too numerous to mention but can be as elaborate or simple as the teacher desires.

Begin by dividing the class into two or three teams by having students "count off" by twos or threes to determine team composition. If students resist this approach, allow them to divide into equal teams of their own choosing, as long as they do it quietly and efficiently in less than 2 minutes. In order to promote student thinking prior to the competition, give students 5 to 10 minutes to work alone to write three questions about the material being studied. The students' questions are then used for the competition and can be turned in to the regular teacher as evidence of the student's thinking.

Be aware that students often become very engaged in such competitions and that classroom noise levels can escalate during the class. This can be controlled in one of three ways:

1. Prior to the competition, make clear that if the noise gets too loud you will give one warning and that the second offense will result termination.

2. Set a rule that "silent cheers" that rely on gesture and facial expression only will be the only form of celebration permitted.

3. Set a rule that any team that gets too loud will lose x number of points from their team score for each offense.

6. **KWL Process.** In this approach to student-centered instruction, the teacher facilitates students in the process of answering three questions designed to promote reflection on their understanding of subject matter. The three questions are: What do you **Know**? What **Would** you like to know? And, What have you **Learned**? The manner in which these three questions are asked, and the way in which students respond, are many and varied. For example, you may want to travel with a preprinted KWL chart that you can pass out to students. Or, you may prefer to simply create three columns on the board and record student responses. Obviously, the first approach is more likely to stimulate personal reflection.

Use students' K column responses to reinforce their existing understanding and praise them for knowledge they currently possess. After discussing students' current knowledge, move the discussion to what they would like to know. Here, students may express general areas of personal interest or curiosity about a topic or may identify areas of knowledge or skill about which they are confused. Use the students' W column entries as springboards to discussions, demonstrations, or forms of additional inquiry aimed at securing the desired knowledge. Use students as important resources in this process, encouraging them to provide insights and information whenever possible. At the end of the class, be sure to leave adequate time to reflect on the class period by completing the L column of the KWL chart. If students are completing their own KWL charts, consider collecting them at the end of the class.

7. **Team Data Analysis.** Begin by providing each student with three 3"x 5" index cards or three medium-size sticky notes. Next, ask students to briefly respond to three questions using a different card for each response. Using color-coded cards or slips of paper is helpful. If not available, collect the cards after each question so that the cards do not become mixed. The three questions can be generated by the students to reflect areas of interest they have about the subject matter. For example, Should the U.S. have used the atomic bomb on Japan? Why or why not? Or, you may use the three generic questions listed below. Instruct students that they do not need to put their name on the cards.

Question #1: What is one thing about the subject matter you are currently studying that is *most confusing* to you? Be as specific as possible.

Question #2: What do you think is the *most important* idea, concept, or skill (adjust the language to the age of students) you are supposed to learn from the subject matter you are studying?

Question #3: What do you find *most interesting* about the current subject matter? After the survey cards are completed, divide the class into three or six teams depending on the size of the class.

If your class consists of twenty-five or fewer students, use three teams; if over twenty-five, use six teams. Provide each team with a set of cards (dividing each set in two if you use six teams). Next, inform the teams that they have 20 minutes to sort and categorize their cards, *analyze the data,* and prepare a brief report for their classmates. Depending on the ages of the students, you will have to provide more or less specific instructions on how they approach the process of data analysis. Encourage students to report any conclusions they feel they can support or any new questions the data raises. Students can be encouraged to use a blackboard or overhead transparency to report their data. You may add further structure to the activity by asking each team to select members to fulfill the roles of reporter, recorder, discussion leader, and so forth.

8. **Visual Diagramming or Mapping.** The purpose of this strategy is to provide students of any age with the opportunity to express their understandings (or misunderstandings) of subject matter by using some form of visual diagram or map. Importantly, such an activity may provide students with artistic ability or visual learners to have the opportunity to experience validation or clearer understanding. Begin by challenging students to think about how they might explain some important understanding about the subject matter they are studying by using a drawing of some sort rather than a verbal explanation. Older students can be encouraged to consider the use of *symbolism* and *metaphor* in their representations.

Divide the class into groups of three to four students and provide each group with a set of common materials to use in their drawing. Depending on availability and preference, you might use poster board, newsprint, or transparency blanks, or simply have each team complete their final drawing on a designated space at the chalkboard. Instruct the teams that they will have 20 minutes to complete their work and prepare for a 3-minute to 5-minute presentation to the class. You may need to adjust the time based on the ages of the students and your observations of their progress.

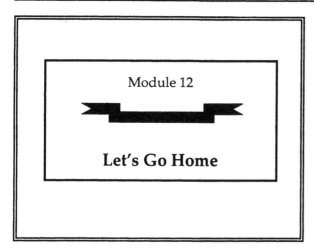

Module 12

Let's Go Home

 Quadrant 3:
Logistical Functions

- **3A:** Understanding and following the rules, procedures, and routines of the school to which one is assigned
- **3B:** Attending efficiently to the non-instructional tasks assigned to the regular teacher
- **3C:** Ensuring that the physical environment of the classroom is left in a clean and orderly condition
- **3D:** Filing end-of-day reports to the regular classroom teacher

---

Criterion 3C

3C: Ensuring that the physical environment of the classroom is left in a clean and orderly condition

3:05

**The Importance of Leaving the Room
Neat and Clean**

Criterion 3D

3D: Filing end-of-day
reports to the
regular classroom
teacher

3:35

**The Importance of Filing
End-of-Day Reports**

End-of-Day Reporting
Do's

✔ Accept them as routine part of job.
✔ Be descriptive, NOT judgmental.
✔ Focus on student learning.
✔ Reference progress on lesson plan(s).
✔ Commend all helpful persons.
✔ Be careful with suggestions or advice.
✔ Include a personal note.

End-of-Day Reporting
Do Nots

✖ Think they aren't necessary
✖ Criticize the teacher
✖ Vent or use "poor me" language
✖ Make judgments
✖ Employ sarcasm
✖ Exaggerate problem situations

Substitute Report

Name
Address
Phone Number

Reflect on the words of advice from the veterans that you have seen in the video clips. Teachers greatly enjoy hearing how the day went, if their plans were understandable, and other important elements. Use a form like this one to leave positive but honest information. Consider personalizing it by creating your own individual stationery.

Module 13

Substitute Teacher as
Professional Person

Quadrant 4:
Professional Functions

■ 4A: Protecting confidential information acquired about
students, parents, teachers, and administrators

■ 4B: Making appropriate referrals to the building
administrator and other professional persons

■ 4C: Consulting with certified and noncertified staff
persons to acquire information or materials to
enhance student learning

■ 4D: Engaging in the processes of reflection and self-
assessment relative to the preceding functions

Criterion 4A

4A: Protecting confidential
information acquired about
students, parents, teachers,
and administrators

3:30

Administrators on Confidentiality

Criterion 4B

4B: Making appropriate referrals to the building administrator and other professional persons

---

Criterion 4C

4C: Consulting with certified and noncertified staff persons to acquire information or materials to enhance student learning

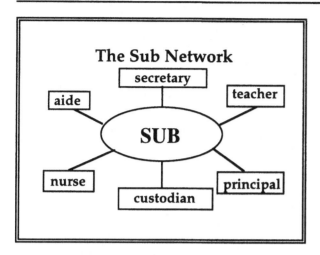

The Sub Network

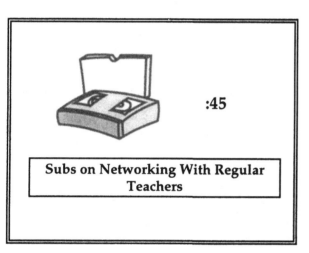

:45

Subs on Networking With Regular Teachers

What Are the Characteristics of Successful Substitutes?

This question was asked of students, faculty members, school administrators, and substitute teachers themselves by researcher Robert Warren (1988).

Warren's Findings

- ❏ Adaptable to various classrooms
- ❏ Are punctual
- ❏ Have knowledge of subject matter
- ❏ Able to manage classroom adversity
- ❏ Possess a sense of humor
- ❏ Able to build rapport with students
- ❏ Have teaching experience

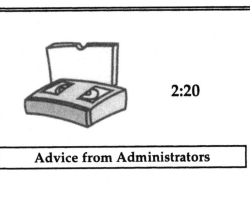

2:20

Advice from Administrators

Advice From School Nurses for Substitute Teachers

1. Do not dispense medication (prescription or over-the-counter) to any of your students. Send them to the building office or school clinic where they will have a record of the written permission to give the child the medication, the prescribed amount, and a system for recording the times and dosage administered.

2. You should refer all students with injuries (even minor ones) to the office so the normal school procedures can be followed. In an emergency, you may need to escort the child to the office. Or, in a less serious situation, have another student accompany the injured child.

3. Carry to school each day a pair of disposable gloves that are waterproof and made of either latex or vinyl, in the event of an emergency that requires you to come in direct contact with a student's injury. School clinics will be able to provide disposable gloves when you arrive at the clinic.

4. Always wear the protective gloves when you come in contact with blood, bodily fluids, and torn skin, or when handling materials soiled with the same.

5. If you come in contact with bodily fluids from a student, throw your gloves away in a lined garbage can. Better yet, first seal the soiled gloves in a small plastic bag before depositing them in the trash. Wash your hands for 10 seconds with soap and warm water after you remove the gloves.

6. Encourage students to wash their hands before meals and when using the rest rooms to reduce exposure to germs.

7. Do not allow students who are bleeding to participate in class until the bleeding has stopped and the wound has been cleaned and completely covered.

8. Check with the school office when there is a student injury. Some schools may require that you complete an accident report form. If so, consider leaving a copy for the teacher whose class you are covering for the day.

9. Prevention is the most important antidote for medical emergencies. Always stay with the children. Contact another adult if you need to leave the students at any time. If you have recess duty, walk around the playground being proactive about potentially dangerous behavior. Remember, you are the adult in charge.

Advice From Special Educators for Substitute Teachers

In some cases, you may be assigned to teach in a special education "resource room" where all of the students have been identified as having special needs. In other cases, you may be teaching in a regular classroom where there are particular students with identified special needs. Whichever is the case, here are some thoughts on how to facilitate the learning of these students.

1. Respect is the key attitude for success with all children.

2. These children may have a variety of learning challenges. Do not think first of their special needs, but think of them first as learners.

3. All children respond to sincere encouragement, but do not overdo it. Be sensitive to the fact that learning is more difficult for these children than for many others.

4. Depending on the grade level you are teaching, these students may have experienced years of school failure. Be aware of that as you respond to their needs and work to help them find success.

5. Depending on the student's learning challenge, you may find you need to repeat yourself more often. Be patient. Check for student understanding after giving directions.

6. If there are problems, do not single out a child in front of the class, but deal with him or her privately.

7. Many children with special needs have Individualized Education Plans (IEPs). Consult these plans when available, as they provide structure for the student's learning. The teacher should have daily plans drawn from these IEPs.

8. You often may be privy to confidential information about children with special needs. It is critical that all information you obtain about children during your teaching day remains confidential. Depending on the grade level, the students may feel self-conscious that you know they have learning challenges, which can set up a defensiveness on their part.

9. During your teaching day, you may need to locate yourself in close proximity to these children to offer assistance and help them stay focused. A gentle reminder will oftentimes suffice for them.

10. An instructional assistant or aide may be in the classroom. Such a person can be of tremendous help because they have a history with the children and are aware of routines, personalities, and other important background information.

11. Do not hesitate to ask for assistance from the principal or another teacher if you have concerns or questions during the day.

12. Carefully note the daily schedules for the special needs children, as they often have support personnel (language or hearing specialists) come into the classroom. At other times, they may leave the classroom to attend regular or special classes.

13. There may be teaching equipment or machines in these classes. Check with the instructional assistant, the principal, or another teacher before using these items.

14. Sometimes children are allowed to use certain learning aids to assist them with their work. Hopefully, the regular teacher will leave information instructing you as to which students may use the aids, and under what circumstances.

15. In some special education classes, behavior reports go home daily to parents that record the behavior of their child throughout the day. Become as familiar as possible with the system, or ask the assistant to focus on giving the feedback for the particular student(s) for the day.

16. In class discussions, if a student responds with an incorrect answer, provide clues or follow-up questions to help him or her think of the correct answer. Look for ways to praise students for their thinking and behavior as well as correct answers.

17. Present short and varied instructional tasks planned with students' success in mind.

18. Have on hand an age-appropriate book to read, audiotapes, flash cards of facts, games, puzzles, mental math exercises, or other activities for substituting in these classes.

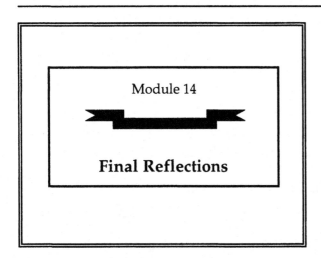

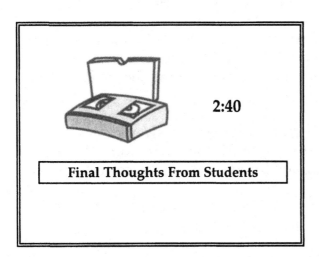

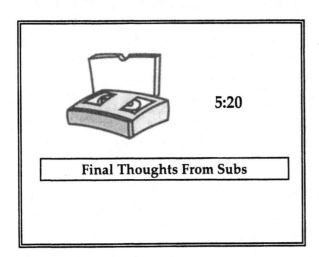

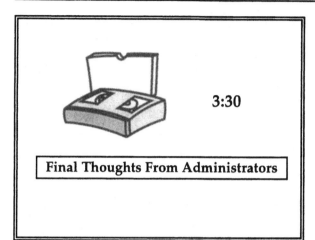

Final Thoughts From Administrators

3:30

"The world can be a better place because you are a teacher. The impact of your influence will never end."

- Madeline Hunter, 1994, p. 245

The End

Resources

The Substitute Teacher Tool Kit

Many substitute teachers find security in traveling to school each day equipped to handle a range of instructional situations and prepared to respond to a variety of minor emergencies. Packing some combination of the following materials in a tote bag, day pack, or briefcase provides the flexibility to be more spontaneous in your teaching and less dependent on having to find a particular material before you can pursue a teaching idea. Consider the following suggestions and add your own ideas to create a personalized *Substitute Teacher Tool Kit.*

Instructional Materials

Clipboard
Index cards
Post-it notes
Overhead transparency blanks
Transparency pens
Spare pencils and pens
Small plastic pencil sharpener
Box of colored chalk
Felt-tip marker
Pocket dictionary
Calculator
Roll of tape
Paper clips
Small stapler and staples
Local daily newspaper or *USA Today*
Favorite book of brainteasers or academic puzzles
Materials needed to deliver a "back-up lesson plan"

Miscellaneous Items

Personalized note pad or stationery (for end-of-day reports)
Log sheet (to keep a record of where and when you worked)
Disposable rubber or vinyl gloves
Pain reliever (for you, not students)
Snack food and drink
Personal items (spare contact lenses, coffee mug, and so forth)

Substitute Teacher Performance Matrix

Quadrant 1: Interpersonal Functions

1A Rapidly establishing an appropriate level of rapport with students

1B Establishing and maintaining student discipline in an environment conducive to teaching and learning

1C Treating all students with respect and with a commitment to fairness

1D Displaying personal enthusiasm and self-confidence when communicating with students

Quadrant 2: Instructional Functions

2A Clearly articulating the goals and procedures of the lesson to be taught

2B Making efficient and meaningful use of instructional time

2C Interpreting, implementing, and enhancing instructional plans prescribed by the regular classroom teacher

2D Employing instructional techniques designed to assess students' prior knowledge and extend student students' thinking

Quadrant 3: Logistical Functions

3A Understanding and following the rules, procedures, and routines of the school to which one is assigned

3B Attending efficiently to the noninstructional tasks assigned to the regular teacher

3C Ensuring that the physical environment of the classroom is left in a clean and orderly condition

3D Filing end-of-day reports to the regular classroom teacher

Quadrant 4: Professional Functions

4A Protecting confidential information acquired about students, parents, teachers, and administrators

4B Making appropriate referrals to the building administrator and other professional persons

4C Consulting with certified and noncertified staff persons to acquire information or materials to enhance student learning

4D Engaging in the processes of reflection and self-assessment relative to the preceding functions

References

Chaney, S. A. (1995). *A handbook for substitute teachers*. Unpublished master's thesis, University of Dayton, Ohio.

Csikszentmihalyi, M. (1978). *Beyond boredom and anxiety*. San Francisco, CA: Jossey-Bass.

Drake, J. M. (1981). Making effective use of the substitute teacher: An administrative opportunity. *NASSP Bulletin, 65*(446), 75.

Gage, N. L. (1978). *The scientific basis of the art of teaching*. New York: Teachers College Press.

Gilson, J. (1982). *Thirteen ways to sink a sub*. New York: Lothrop, Lee, & Shepard.

Glickman, C. D., & Tamashiro, R. T. (1980). Clarifying teachers' beliefs about discipline. *Educational Leadership, 37*(6), 459-465.

Hunter, M. (1994). *Enhancing teaching*. New York: Macmillan.

Johnson, D. W. (1993). *Reaching out* (5th ed.). Needham Heights, MA: Allyn & Bacon.

Koelling, C. H. (1983). Substitute teachers -- School policies and procedures in the North Central Region. *Education, 104*(2), 163.

Maslow, A. H. (1954). *Motivation and personality*. New York: Harper & Brothers.

McIntire, R. G., & Hughes, L. W. (1982, June). Houston program trains effective substitutes. *Phi Delta Kappan, 63*(10), 702.

Pronin, B. (1983). Guerrilla guide to effective substitute teaching. *Instructor, 92*(6), 65-68.

Pronin, B. (1983). *Substitute teaching: A handbook for hassle-free subbing*. New York: St. Martin's.

St. Michel, T. (1995). *Effective substitute teachers: Myth, mayhem, or magic?* Thousand Oaks, CA: Corwin.

Warren, R. (1988). Substitute teachers -- Education's relief pitchers. *NASSP Bulletin, 72*(512), 96.

Suggested Readings

Aceto, J. T. (1995). A piece of cake. *Phi Delta Kappan,76*(6), 490, 492.

Ban, J. R. (1990). Help substitute teachers manage student behavior. *Executive Educator, 12*(2), 24-25.

Bartolotta, M., Samuels, S., & Nidds, J. A. (1994). Substitute teachers: Seeking meaningful instruction in the teacher's absence. *The Clearing House, 68*, 25-26.

Billman, L. W. (1994). Keep subs afloat. *Executive Educator, 16*, 29-31.

Blachowicz, C. L. Z., Bartolotta, M., & Samuels, S. (1993). Subframe: A strategic planning frame for substitute teachers. *Journal of Reading, 37*(3), 234-235.

Brill, A. (1992). *Substitute teaching: Problems and recommendations.* Unpublished doctoral dissertation, Indiana University, Bloomington.

Buchberg, W., Wayman, M., Choat, D., & Gotliffe, A. (1995). Teachers' help-one-another club. Management advice for substitutes. *Instructor, 104*(7), 12.

Charles, C. M., & Senter, G. W. (1992). *Building classroom discipline* (4th ed.). White Plains, NY: Longman.

Dilanian, S. M. (1986). Dimensions of needs in secondary substitute teaching. EDRS Availability #ED277686.

Dubois, M., Gangel, K., Young, L., Heiss, R., Webb, B., & Paprocki, S. (1991). The canvas bag and other substitute survival strategies. *Instructor, 101*(1), 54-57.

Ferrara, P. J., & Ferrara, M. M. (1993). Where's our real teacher? *Schools in the Middle, 3*(2), 11-15.

Fielder, D. J. (1991). An examination of substitute teacher effectiveness. *The Clearing House, 64*, 375-377.

Fuller, F. (1969). Concerns of teachers: A developmental conceptualization. *American Educational Research Journal, 6*, 207-226.

Garwood, S. G. (1976). Ten ways to prevent classroom chaos. *Grade Teacher, 94*(2), 75.

Goldenhersh, B. L. (1995). *The effect of a course on substitute teaching on stage of concern, attitude, and experience of substitute teachers*. Unpublished doctoral dissertation, Southern Illinois University, Carbondale.

Goldenhersh, B. L., & Divins, B. J. (1998). *Being an effective substitute teacher*. Salt Lake City: Utah State Press.

Gunderson, M., Snyder, R., & Hillen, B. (1985). Keep your sub from sinking! *Instructor, 95*(2), 160-162.

Johnson, J. M., Holcombe, M., & Vance, K. (1988). Apprehensions of substitute teachers. *The Clearing House, 62*(2), 89-91.

Jones, C. A. (1998). *Substitute teacher's reference manual* (2nd ed.). Palm Springs, CA: ETC Publications.

Kaufmann, F. A. (Ed.). (1991). *Substitute teachers' lesson plans: Classroom-tested activities from the National Council of Teachers of English*. Urbana, IL: The Council.

Lale, M. (1977). Save your sub's sanity: Ways to prepare for a possible absence. *Instructor, 86*(7), 95.

Lovley, S. (1994). A practical guide to substituting at different grade levels. *Pre K-8, 25*(2), 70-71.

Manera, E. S. (1992). A training model for the substitute teacher. *Contemporary Education, 63*, 287-290.

Manera, E. S. (1996). *Substitute teaching: Planning for success*. West Lafayette, IN: Kappa Delta Pi.

Manera, E. S., & Quinn, C. (1991). *The forgotten professional: The substitute teacher*. Paper presented at the annual meeting of the Rocky Mountain Education Research Association, El Paso, Texas.

Maytray, K. (1993). Just a matter of time -- SuperSubs for staff development. *The Computing Teacher, 21*(1), 12, 14.

McGillian, J. K. (1995, August). Give your sub a break! Ideas, advice, and reproducibles. *Creative Classroom*, 75-89.

McKay, P. (1991). Survival tactics for a substitute (Sob! Sob!) teacher. *The Clearing House, 64*, 331-333.

McMillan, M. (1992). *Lifesavers for substitutes: A wealth of ideas for the classroom teacher as well*. Carthage, IL: Good Apple.

Molk, C. J. R. (1990). *A handbook for substitute teachers*. Unpublished master's thesis, University of Dayton, Ohio.

Nidds, J. A., & McGerald, J. (1994). Substitute teachers: Seeking meaningful instruction in the teacher's absence. *The Clearing House, 68*(1), 25-26.

Peterson, S. (1991). An action plan for training substitute teachers. *The Clearing House, 65*, 37-38.

Pitkoff, E. (1989). "Sub" policies or sub-policies? A look at policies pertaining to substitute teaching programs. *American Secondary Education, 17*(4), 17-20.

Platt, J. M. (1987). Substitute teachers can do more than just keep the lid on. *Teaching Exceptional Children, 19*(2), 28-31.

Presberg, H. (1988). Accept no substitute (for good substitute teaching). *Science and Children, 26*(1), 26-28.

Purvis, J. P., & Garvey, R. C. (1993). Components of an effective substitute teacher program. *The Clearing House, 66*(6), 370-373.

Rosborough, M., Sherbine, D., & Miller, D. (1993). Recruiting, selecting, and training substitute teachers. *NASSP Bulletin, 76*(550), 104-106.

Shepherd, R. L. (1997). Formative assessment for substitute teachers. *The Clearing House, 71*, 117-118.

Simmons, B. J. (1991). Planning to improve the quality of the substitute teacher program. *NASSP Bulletin, 75*, 91-98.

Stanley, S. (1991). Substitute teachers can manage their classrooms effectively. *NASSP Bulletin, 75*(532), 84-88.

Swick, K. J. (1991). *Discipline: Toward posititve student behavior--What research says to the teacher*. Washington, DC: National Education Association Professional Library.

Tracey, S. J. (1988). Improve substitute teaching with staff development. *NASSP Bulletin, 72*(508), 85-88.

Videon, L., McDuffie, C., & Stopper, J. (1987). *Take me along: The best substitute teacher's survival guide yet!* Belmont, CA: David S. Lake.

Westling, D. L., & Koorland, M. A. (1988). *The special educator's handbook*. Boston: Allyn & Bacon.

Wilson, K. G. (1985). Guidelines for substitute teachers in secondary schools. *NASSP Bulletin, 69*(479), 73-76.

Wong, H. K., & Wong, R. T. (1991). *The first days of school.* Sunnyvale, CA: H. K. Wong.

Woods, L. L., & Woods, T. L. (1974). Substitutes: A psychological study. *Elementary School Journal, 75,* 163-167.

More resources from Corwin Press

"This book is wonderful. All teachers will benefit from the in-depth coverage and the invaluable checklists on how to set up a classroom and keep it functioning so that everyone meets with success."

Karleen D. Hamilton, Teacher, El Rancho Structured School, Camarillo, California

1995, 128 pages, 4th printing!
D8818-6288-6 (Library Edition)   **$41.95**   **D8818-6289-4** (Paper)   **$18.00**

Practical strategies you can use immediately.
1998, 120 pages
D8818-6604-0 (Paper)   **$17.95**
D8818-6603-2 (Lib. Ed.)   **$41.95**

"On target! A bull's-eye view of the classroom experience."

Linda Goldberg, Teacher Trainer/Staff Developer
New York City

1997, 136 pages, 2nd printing!
D8818-6556-7 (Paper)   **$17.95**
D8818-6555-9 (Library Edition)   **$41.95**

"Here is a commonsense, practical approach to good discipline. Well-organized, logical, and sequential, it's like having a toolbox filled with tools."
Curt Boudreaux, Retired Principal,
Education and Business Consultant
1995, 128 pages, 8½" x 11" Workbook
2nd printing!
D8818-6341-6 (Paper)   **$22.95**

"Want to love your job again? Give yourself and your students this gift! It's full of wisdom, inspiration, and practical information."

Rebecca Merriman
Educator, Author of *Simply Free*
1998, 96 pages
D8818-6721-7 (Paper)   **$14.95**
D8818-6720-9 (Library Edition)   **$35.95**

"A wonderful collection of practical advice. Must reading for new and continuing teachers."
Bonnie Blum, Director of Student Services, Azusa Unified School District, California
1998, 112 pages
D8818-6728-4 (Library Edition)   **$35.95**   **D8818-6729-2** (Paper)   **$14.95**

CORWIN PRESS, INC.
A Sage Publications Company
2455 Teller Road
Thousand Oaks, CA 91320-2218
Federal ID Number 77-0260569

ORDER FORM

D8818

(For faster service, photocopy this form and send with your P.O.)

(Professional books may be tax-deductible.)

Easy Ways to Order

- **Call: 805-499-9774**
- **Fax this form to: 805-499-0871**
- **Mail your completed order form**
- **E-mail us at: order@corwinpress.com**

Ship to
Name / Title _____
Institution _____
Address_____ #_____
City _____ State _____ ZIP + 4_____
Country_____
Telephone (_____) _____
P.O. # _____
(Actual purchase order must be attached.)

Method of Payment

☐ Check enclosed # _____   ☐ VISA   ☐ MC   ☐ DISCOVER

Account Number _____ Exp. Date _____

Signature _____

Qty.	Book No.	Title	Unit Price	Amount

*Domestic shipping and handling charges are $3.50 for the first book and $1.00 for each additional book. These charges apply to all orders, including purchase orders and those prepaid by check or credit card. All orders are shipped Ground Parcel unless otherwise requested. Prices subject to change without notice. International handling charges are $6.00 for the first item and $3.00 for each additional item. In Canada, add $10.00 for the first item and $2.00 for each additional item. Please add 7% GST (12978 6448 RT) and remit in U.S. dollars. Thank you.

Total Order	
In IL, add 6¼% sales tax	
In MA, add 5% sales tax	
In NY and CA, add appropriate sales tax	
In Canada, add 7% GST*	
Subtotal	
Handling Charges*	
Amount Due	

Printed in the United States
By Bookmasters